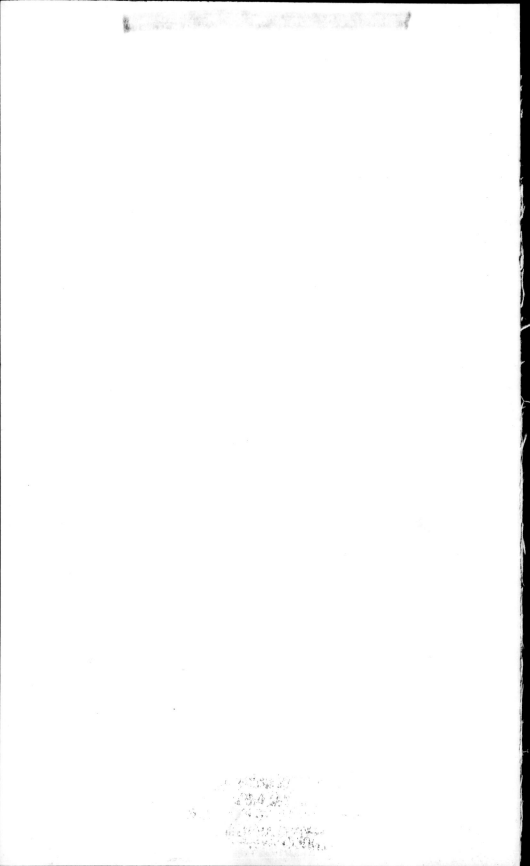

This gerbil is a spy.

TRUE or FALSE?

CONFIDENTIAL

CONFIDENTIAL

TRUE!

Well, not this gerbil, exactly.

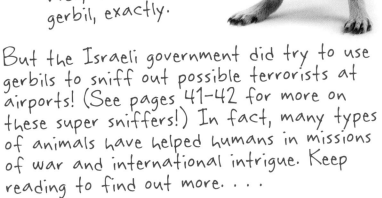

But the Israeli government did try to use gerbils to sniff out possible terrorists at airports! (See pages 41–42 for more on these super sniffers!) In fact, many types of animals have helped humans in missions of war and international intrigue. Keep reading to find out more. . . .

Book design Red Herring Design/NYC

Library of Congress Cataloging-in-Publication Data
Denega, Danielle, 1978–
The Cold War pigeon patrols: and other animal spies / by Danielle Denega.
p. cm. — (24/7:Science Behind the Scenes)
Includes bibliographical references and index.
ISBN-13: 978-0-531-12081-1 (lib. bdg.)   978-0-531-17534-7 (pbk.)
ISBN-10: 0-531-12081-3 (lib. bdg.)   0-531-17534-0 (pbk.)
1. Espionage—Juvenile literature. 2. Spies—Juvenile literature. 3. Animals—War use—Juvenile literature. I. Title.
UB270.5.D45 2007
327.1209'045—dc22   2006005869

© 2008 Scholastic Inc.
All rights reserved. Published by Franklin Watts, an imprint of Scholastic Inc.

Published simultaneously in Canada. Printed in the United States of America.

SCHOLASTIC, FRANKLIN WATTS, and associated logos are trademarks and/or registered trademarks of Scholastic Inc.
1 2 3 4 5 6 7 8 9 10 R 17 16 15 14 13 12 11 10 09 08
AUG 2 4 2009

THE COLD WAR
PIGEON PATROLS

And Other Animal Spies

Danielle Denega

WARNING: This book contains true-life stories. They all involve real spy animals. Some of these animals were hurt or killed in the line of duty.

Franklin Watts
An Imprint of Scholastic Inc.
New York • Toronto • London • Auckland • Sydney
Mexico City • New Delhi • Hong Kong
Danbury, Connecticut

CONTENTS

SPY 411

Before you snoop through the case files, read this section to get all the secret info about spies.

4

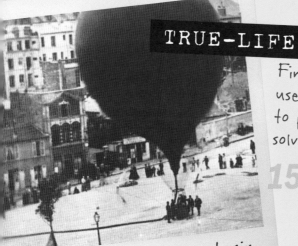

Find out how animal spies use their top-secret powers to protect humans and solve crimes.

Why were pigeons in hot-air balloons in Paris?

These super-intelligent animals saved lives in Iraq.

Bloodhounds and other super sniffers are on the prowl.

5

Not all spies walk on two legs. Some of history's most successful sleuths fly, bark, and swim.

SPY 411

That's right. Animals have become undercover heroes in the military, on the police force, and even in the CIA. These are their stories.

IN THIS SECTION:

▶ how animal handlers really talk;

▶ the hidden talents of animal agents;

▶ and who else is part of the spy team.

Undercover Speak

Experts who work with animals have their own way of speaking. Find out what their vocabulary means.

handler
(HAN-dler) a person responsible for training and caring for animals

agent
(AY-juhnt) a person or animal who collects information and performs other secret tasks for an intelligence service like the CIA

mission
(MIH-shun) a special job or task

espionage
(ESS-pee-uh-nahzh) the act of spying or the work of a spy

spy
(spye) a person or animal who secretly gets or sends information

intelligence
(in-TEL-uh-juhnss) information gained by spying

I'm the **handler** of these animal **agents**. What's their next **mission**?

Since you're an expert in **espionage**, send the **spy** out to gather **intelligence**.

> Okay, we'll send the agent across enemy lines. Once he gets the information, he'll deliver it to the allies.

enemy
(EN-uh-mee) the "bad guys"; the side you're fighting against

allies
(AL-eyes) the "good guys"; the people or groups on your side

> Are you worried about the enemy's counterintelligence group?

counterintelligence
(kown-ter-in-TEL-uh-juhnss) organized activity that catches spies or blocks the transfer of information between spies and intelligence agencies

Say What?

Here's some other lingo an animal spy trainer might use on the job.

rafts
(rafts) large groups of dead skin cells that fall off a person's body. Tracking dogs follow rafts to find missing people.
*"I think Fido has sniffed out the missing boy's **rafts**. It's only a matter of time now until he tracks the boy down."*

scent receptors
(SENT reh-SEP-turz) the sensitive places inside the nose that tell your brain what you smell
*"Did you know that a dog has about 44 times the number of **scent receptors** a human has?"*

sonar
(SO-nahr) a way of locating objects underwater by using sound waves
*"Did you see how quickly that dolphin found the coin we threw in the water? Its **sonar** is amazing."*

A Spy's Best Friend

Here's a look at the natural abilities that have helped these animals go undercover.

Animal Spy Pigeons
Service Military
Skill Homing. Some pigeons can be trained to return home after traveling distances of 500 miles (805 km) or more.
Missions They carried messages across enemy lines during the Franco-Prussian War (1870–1871), World War I (1914–1918), and World War II (1939–1945).

Animal Spy Dolphins
Service Military
Skill Sonar. Dolphins send sound waves from their brains to identify objects in the water.
Missions They have discovered mines and other explosives during the Iraq War.

Animal Spy Dogs
Service Police, military, and intelligence agencies like the **CIA**
Skill Super sniffing. Dogs have a superhuman sense of smell. Their noses can be 44 times more powerful than a human's.
Missions They find hidden bombs and drugs and track missing people.

Animal Spy Gerbils
Service International airport security
Skill Super sniffing. Gerbils are able to smell when people are nervous or afraid. How? They can **detect** an increase in humans' **adrenaline**.
Missions They detected possible **terrorists** at the Tel Aviv airport in Israel.

Animal Spy Peregrine falcon
Service Military
Skill Super flying. Peregrine falcons are the fastest animals in the world.
Missions They caught and killed Nazi homing pigeons in World War II.

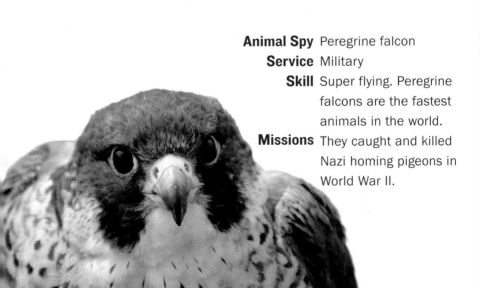

The Spy Team

In the U.S., thousands of people work in intelligence. Their job is to provide information about threats to national security.

OPERATIONS OFFICERS

They're spies. They work with foreign contacts and sources that provide tips and information. Much of their work is focused on terrorism.

LANGUAGE OFFICERS

They support agents in the field as translators and interpreters. Their knowledge of foreign cultures is important to the success of any mission.

DIRECTOR OF NATIONAL INTELLIGENCE

This person and his or her staff coordinate all the different intelligence agencies. A member of this staff briefs the president every morning about intelligence issues.

COLLECTION MANAGEMENT OFFICERS

They guide operations officers to make sure they gather the kind of information that intelligence officials in Washington need. They often work undercover.

ANALYSTS

They take intelligence that comes in from all over the globe and figure out its importance and value. Many focus on trying to understand the plans of terrorist groups.

ENGINEERS AND SCIENTISTS

These are the people who design and operate the systems and gadgets that allow agents to locate, track, and record people.

TRUE-LIFE CASE FILES!

24 hours a day, 7 days a week, 365 days a year, spy agencies, police forces, and the military are on alert. And as part of their missions, they are bringing undercover animal agents to the rescue.

IN THIS SECTION:

- ▶ homing pigeons become wartime spy heroes;
- ▶ two brave dolphins save lives in the Iraq War;
- ▶ dogs and gerbils sniff out some bad guys!

TMI?

Is there Too Much Information to keep track of? Here's a look at some of the top agencies in the U.S. that gather and keep track of intelligence.

CIA

Created in 1947, the Central Intelligence Agency is America's leading spy organization. The CIA gathers information about foreign threats to the U.S.

FBI

The Federal Bureau of Investigation looks into terrorism and collects foreign counterintelligence in the U.S. The FBI also combats organized crime and other criminal activities in the U.S. More than 30,000 people work for the FBI.

NSA

The National Security Agency is a branch of the U.S. Department of Defense. It's responsible for the security of U.S. government communications. It may also break into the communications of other countries. The NSA is home to code breakers who figure out the contents of secret messages.

DIA

The Defense Intelligence Agency is a branch of the U.S. Department of Defense. It provides analysis and support to the military. Its mission includes everything from advising generals on combat strategy to collecting intelligence about foreign leaders.

DHS

The Department of Homeland Security is responsible for protecting the United States. It provides terrorist alerts. It watches for storms like the killer Hurricane Katrina. And it advises local and state governments on safety measures.

1870-Today

Spy Pigeons Go to War

The humble homing pigeon becomes a
battlefield hero. Find out about
its undercover exploits.

The Siege of Paris: 1870

Can homing pigeons help the French Army survive a deadly battle?

It was July 1870, and France's military leaders were trapped in Paris. German troops had surrounded the city. Paris was under **siege**. How would the trapped French generals communicate with their armies outside of Paris?

They came up with a brilliant plan. They'd use homing pigeons as spies to carry messages from the soldiers. Homing pigeons are bred to fly long distances, and then find their way home again. Some can travel more than 1,500 miles (2,400 km) before returning home!

The French generals put the pigeons in hot-air balloons and sent them out of Paris. The balloons flew high over the enemy. Soon, the balloons reached French troops in different parts of the country.

The soldiers freed the pigeons from the balloons. Then they wrote messages back to their leaders in Paris.

When French generals were trapped inside Paris, they had pigeons placed in hot-air balloons like this one and sent to their armies outside the city. Soldiers then sent messages back to Paris, informing the generals about the enemy's activities.

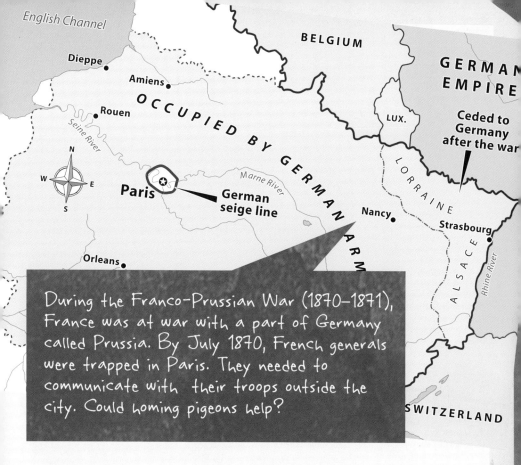

English Channel

BELGIUM

Dieppe

Amiens

Rouen

OCCUPIED BY GERMAN ARMY

GERMAN EMPIRE

LUX.

Ceded to Germany after the war

LORRAINE

Seine River

Marne River

Paris

German seige line

Nancy

Strasbourg

ALSACE

Rhine River

Orleans

SWITZERLAND

During the Franco-Prussian War (1870–1871), France was at war with a part of Germany called Prussia. By July 1870, French generals were trapped in Paris. They needed to communicate with their troops outside the city. Could homing pigeons help?

They explained what the enemy army was doing. They put the messages in small tubes and attached them to the pigeons' legs. Then they let the birds go.

The pigeons flew home to Paris—just as they were supposed to! The French generals were thrilled when the birds arrived. They read the messages their soldiers had sent. They learned what the enemy was up to— and prepared new battle plans.

The Siege of Paris lasted four months. During that time, about 400 homing pigeons were sent. And thousands of messages got through.

Sadly, fewer than 100 pigeons survived the war. The Germans soon realized the birds were helping the French leaders get important information. So they began shooting them down.

In the end, the Germans won the war. But the homing pigeons had helped the French survive the Siege of Paris.

HOW DO PIGEONS FIND THEIR WAY HOME?

Homing pigeons naturally return to where they live. They can be taken hundreds of miles away and still find their way home. That's why they are called *homing* pigeons!

The pigeons can travel more than 500 miles (805 km) in a single day. In fact, researchers have tracked pigeon flights of more than 1,600 miles (2,600 km) at a time. Homing pigeons fly 30 miles per hour (48 kph), but can reach 60 miles per hour (97 kph) in short bursts.

Scientists still don't know exactly how these special birds find their way home. Some researchers think homing pigeons follow the **magnetic pull** of the earth's North and South poles. Others think the birds are guided by the sun. Still others believe the birds can identify landmarks, like rivers—or even highways.

Bloody Verdun: 1918

Can one homing pigeon save the lives of 200 American soldiers?

A bloody battle was raging near Verdun, France. It was October 3, 1918. World War I was in full swing.

More than 500 American soldiers were trapped on a French hillside. They were surrounded by German soldiers with grenades and machine guns. And American bombs were falling on them by mistake!

When the first day of the battle ended, only 200 Americans were still alive or unhurt. They needed help—and fast! But how would they get a message past the enemy?

Luckily, they had three homing pigeons. They sent the first bird with a message attached: "Many wounded. We cannot

This World War I soldier is attaching a message to a pigeon. These birds were used to help troops communicate during the war.

In October 1918, one of the deadliest battles of World War I was fought near Verdun, France. A homing pigeon named Cher Ami helped save 200 American lives.

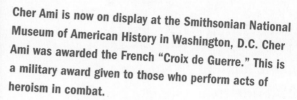

Cher Ami is now on display at the Smithsonian National Museum of American History in Washington, D.C. Cher Ami was awarded the French "Croix de Guerre." This is a military award given to those who perform acts of heroism in combat.

According to some stories, just before World War I, an inventor made a small camera that automatically took photos. His plan was to attach this camera to a pigeon and have it take photos behind enemy lines.

evacuate." The pigeon was shot down by the Germans. They sent the second bird with the message: "Men are suffering. Can support be sent?" That pigeon was shot down, too!

The Americans only had one homing pigeon left. Its name was Cher Ami, which means "Dear Friend" in French.

Cher Ami was released with this message: "We are along the road parallel to 276.4. Our own **artillery** is dropping a **barrage** directly on us. For heaven's sake, stop it."

The Germans saw Cher Ami and opened fire. The bird was hit in the chest by a bullet and fell. The Americans were crushed! Cher Ami had been their last hope.

Then miraculously, Cher Ami was able to spread its wings and fly again. It darted past the enemy fire. Wounded, Cher Ami managed to fly 25 miles (40 km) in only 25 minutes. The pigeon delivered its message!

The bombing stopped. Reinforcements came. More than 200 American lives were saved by this homing pigeon!

Nazi Pigeon Invasion: 1942

When the enemy uses homing pigeons as spies, British intelligence trains a new airborne secret agent.

The British had been fighting in World War II for more than a year. Led by Adolf Hitler's Nazi Party, Germany had already conquered many European countries. Hundreds of thousands of people had died. And now the Nazis wanted to **invade** Britain!

The British spy agency, MI5, was on alert for unusual activity. One day, someone there noticed something suspicious. Homing pigeons were flying in and out of Great Britain.

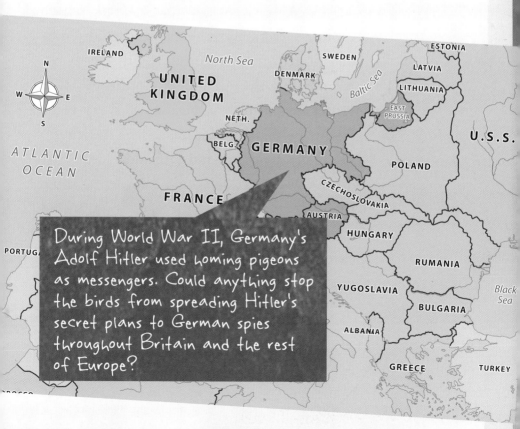

During World War II, Germany's Adolf Hitler used homing pigeons as messengers. Could anything stop the birds from spreading Hitler's secret plans to German spies throughout Britain and the rest of Europe?

During World War II, a British spy agency used peregrine falcons like this one to hunt down Nazi-trained pigeons.

An investigation followed. These birds didn't belong to the British. They were Nazi pigeons!

The MI5 went to the prisons where captured German soldiers were held. They questioned the prisoners about the birds. Eventually, the prisoners confessed that Hitler was using the pigeons to carry plans for his invasions to German spies in Britain, Germany, Belgium, and Holland.

The MI5 was determined to defeat these flying Nazi spies. So the agency **recruited** some birds of a very different feather: peregrine falcons. Peregrine falcons make great hunters because they are the fastest animals in the world. And they can change direction in an instant.

The MI5 trained the peregrines to hunt

Nazi pigeons. Teams of falcons would patrol the sky in two-hour shifts off the British coast. They would **intercept** and kill any pigeons they spotted.

The falcons were so successful at stopping Hitler's secret messages, they became national heroes.

The Cold War Pigeon Patrol: 1947

After World War II, a British spy agency creates a plan for poisonous pigeon attacks on the enemy.

Starting in 1947, there was a period in history called the **Cold War**. It was a conflict between democratic countries like the U.S. and communist countries like the Soviet Union. Both sides had **nuclear weapons**, so everyone was afraid. Spies were everywhere!

During that time, the British intelligence agency MI5 created a secret "pigeon committee." Its goal was to find new ways to use the birds as spies. "If we do not experiment, other powers will," one agency leader wrote about the pigeon plan.

The British had used pigeons as spies during World War II (*shown here*). During the Cold War, British intelligence services again tried to send pigeons back on patrol. The plan was eventually canceled.

So what was the pigeon committee's idea? They wanted to train the birds to fly into enemy territory with small explosive devices strapped to their backs. Inside the devices would be a deadly poison. When the pigeons landed, the devices would explode, releasing the poison to kill the enemy. "A thousand pigeons, each with a two-ounce (57-g) explosive might be a seriously inconvenient surprise," wrote one military leader.

Of course, the pigeons would be killed, too.

Some British officials thought this was a great idea. Others disagreed.

In the end, the plan never happened. It was too expensive. The government decided there were better ways to spend their money for training spies. 24/7

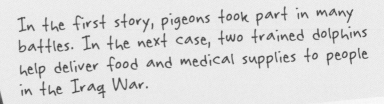

In the first story, pigeons took part in many battles. In the next case, two trained dolphins help deliver food and medical supplies to people in the Iraq War.

The Persian Gulf
2003

Underwater Agents

Two military dolphins
search for deadly underwater
mines. The lives of many Iraqi
civilians depend on their success.

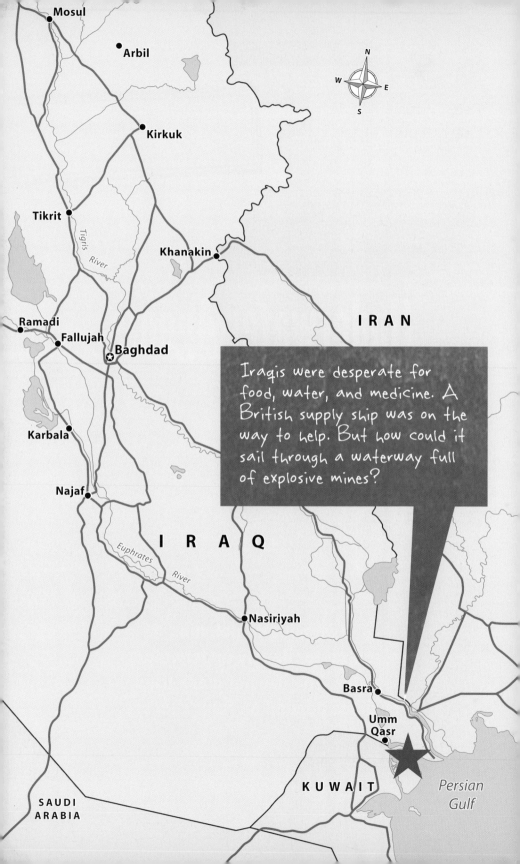

Mosul

Arbil

Kirkuk

Tikrit

Tigris River

Khanakin

Ramadi

Fallujah

Baghdad

Karbala

Najaf

Euphrates River

I R A Q

Nasiriyah

Basra

Umm Qasr

KUWAIT

SAUDI ARABIA

I R A N

Persian Gulf

N
W E
S

Iraqis were desperate for food, water, and medicine. A British supply ship was on the way to help. But how could it sail through a waterway full of explosive mines?

Beware of the Deadly Mines!

People badly need food and water. But how can a supply ship sail into the mine-filled port?

In March 2003, the war in Iraq was raging. People were dying. Iraqi men, women, and children were in desperate need of food and medical supplies.

The British ship *Sir Galahad* was headed toward the Iraqi port of Umm Qasr. On board were 100 tons of water and 150 tons of rice, lentils, sugar, powdered milk, medicine, and other supplies.

But there was one big problem: The water was full of explosive **mines**!

If the supply ship hit one of these mines, it would blow up, and the ship might sink. That meant the mines had to be found and destroyed before the ship could enter the port and unload its supplies.

U.S. and British military teams were brought in to search for the mines. There were more than 50 divers hunting for the deadly devices by hand in dark, muddy water. The divers found it impossible to see what they were doing. Their lives were at risk.

But was there another solution to this dangerous mission?

Yes, bring in the dolphins!

Sir Galahad, a British supply ship, arrives in the Iraqi port city of Umm Qasr on March 23, 2003. The ship was delivering the first shipment of humanitarian supplies since the war began.

Mammals are animals that:
▶ have lungs and breath air
▶ are warm-blooded and have a constant body temperature
▶ give birth to live young
▶ produce milk and nurse their young
▶ have hair at some point in their lives

A marine mammal is simply a mammal that lives in water!

The bottlenose dolphin is a marine mammal that has been used by the U.S. Navy for special missions.

Underwater Agents

Why do dolphins make good spies?

The U.S. Navy trains **marine mammals**, such as dolphins, to help in deadly situations like the one in Iraq. The U.S. Navy Marine Mammal Program is located in San Diego, California. There, the Navy does research, development, and training on how marine mammals, like dolphins, can help humans.

In the late 1950s, the Navy began to study the special traits of dolphins. Navy scientists thought that by understanding why dolphins swim so well, they might be able to improve ship and submarine designs.

But the Navy scientists quickly realized that dolphins could also assist divers working in the ocean. They have an amazing ability to find objects in the water.

That's because dolphins have the best sonar known to humans. Sonar is a way of locating objects by using sound waves. A dolphin's brain sends out sound waves that hit the underwater object and bounce back. That lets the dolphin know where the object is. A dolphin can locate an object the size of a quarter from 100 feet (30 m) away!

Because of their powerful sonar, dolphins were first used to find mines in the 1970s during the Vietnam War. Now it was time for them to find mines in Iraq.

These deadly mines were cleared from the shipping lanes of the port city of Umm Qasr in Iraq.

MAKING SOUND WAVES
Dolphins use sonar to detect objects underwater.

Dolphins are able to locate mines by using their natural sonar. Sonar is a way of using sound waves to find objects.

Here's how it works:

Dolphins produce sounds called **clicks**. These clicks pass through special structures in their brains called **melons**. The melon focuses these clicks into beams of sound waves.

These sound waves move out in front of the dolphin. When they hit an object, the sound waves bounce off the object and return to the dolphin as **echoes**.

The dolphin receives this echo in the fat-filled part of its lower jaw. The sound is then sent to the ear and the brain.

Echo, Echo, Echo

As a dolphin gets closer to an object, the clicks and echoes happen more often. The echoes form a pattern. This pattern is called an **echolocation** pattern. *Echo* means to repeat; *location* is where something can be found.

Dolphins are able to form a mental picture based on an object's echolocation pattern. That's how they know where to find the object.

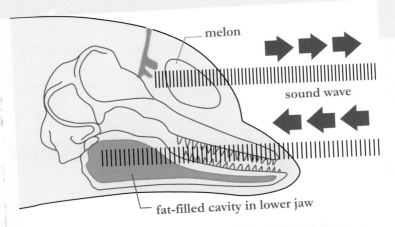

melon

sound wave

fat-filled cavity in lower jaw

Dolphins make sounds called clicks. The sound waves from these clicks bounce off objects and echo back to the dolphins. This process allows the dolphins to use sound waves to find objects.

Dolphins to the Rescue

Two bottlenose dolphins search for deadly mines in the port of Umm Qasr, Iraq.

Makai and Tacoma were two of the specially trained dolphins flown to the Persian Gulf to locate deadly mines in the port of Umm Qasr.

Makai was 33 years old, and Tacoma was 22 years old. Both were male Atlantic bottlenose dolphins. They were trained at the U.S. Navy Marine Mammal Program in San Diego, California.

Makai and Tacoma were taught to find mines by using their sonar. Once they found a mine, they were trained to avoid danger by never touching the deadly device!

Instead, they would place buoys, or floats, around the mines. All the people and animals would be moved very far away from the exploding mines so no one was hurt. Then humans who were explosives experts would safely blow up the mines.

A sergeant from the U.S. Navy transports a bottlenose dolphin named K-Dog in March 2003. This dolphin has been trained to find dangerous mines in Iraqi waters.

Now it was time for Makai and Tacoma to get to work. They had to find all the hidden mines so the supply ship could sail safely into the port.

DOLPHIN DEBATE

Some animal rights activists want the military to stop using marine mammals.

Not everyone thinks the U.S. Navy should train dolphins and other marine mammals.

An animal-rights group called People for the Ethical Treatment of Animals (PETA) is against the use of dolphins by the military. Stephanie Boyles, a PETA wildlife biologist, says dolphins shouldn't be forced to be part of the U.S. Navy's Marine Mammal Program.

Dolphins "don't realize the tasks they are being taught to perform are life-and-death," Boyles says. "They think this is a game, and yet the risk to their lives and the amount of suffering they may endure is great. We don't seem to care about that."

Military dolphins are kept in tanks of water. They have less room to move than they would have in the ocean. This can cause them extreme mental and physical stress. These dolphins can be more aggressive and live shorter lives than they would in the wild.

What Do You Think?

The U.S. Navy says that all its dolphins are well taken care of and aren't put in danger. They help save human lives.

It's a tough issue to decide. What do you think? Should the Navy stop training dolphins and other marine mammals to help humans?

Mission Accomplished!

Makai and Tacoma help uncover six deadly mines. And the badly needed supplies are finally delivered.

For a week, Makai and Tacoma worked hard searching for mines. They had a large area to cover. The waterway into the port was 200 yards (183 m) wide and 40 miles (64 km) long!

They swam for hours at a time. They used their amazing sonar to hunt for mines. Whenever they located an object, they swam closer to inspect it.

Sometimes it was nothing but a passing school of fish. Or it was just some trash, like an empty oil barrel.

But when Makai and Tacoma found a mine, they were careful not to get too close. They marked the mine with buoys, as they were trained. Then their human handlers safely exploded the device.

At the end of the week, they had found six mines.

Thanks to Makai and Tacoma, the waterway was now safe to travel. The supply ship, *Sir Galahad*, docked at the port of Umm Qasr. Crew members unloaded the 100 tons of water and 150 tons of food. They also unloaded blankets, medicine, and other emergency supplies.

The Iraqi people were finally getting the supplies they needed. 24/7

K-Dog, a trained bottlenose dolphin, leaps out of the water in front of a U.S. sergeant. The device attached to the dolphin's fin is a "pinger." That allows his handlers to keep track of him when he's out of sight.

[Now Hear This]
The Navy is developing robots to search for mines. But the robots are no match for dolphin sonar. A dolphin's hearing is much more sensitive than any robot. In fact, the only animal on earth with a better sense of hearing than the dolphin is the bat.

REMOTE-CONTROL SPY SHARKS

Can a marine professor turn Jaws into an undercover agent?

In his lab, Jelle Atema is studying a 3-foot (0.9 m) dogfish shark. Atema is a professor with the Boston University Marine Program.

This is no ordinary shark. Atema has attached electrical wires to different places on its skull. Why? To steer the shark by remote control!

Sharks love the smell of blood in the water. It means dinnertime. When Atema turns on the electric current, the shark's sense of smell kicks into gear. The shark thinks it smells blood.

Atema's goal is to steer the shark like a remote-control car—only in the ocean!

If Atema succeeds, the military could use these remote-control sharks to swim through dangerous waters. They could wear **sensors** that detect mines and explosives. That way, human divers wouldn't be at risk.

Or the sharks could wear cameras. These remote-control spy sharks could be sent to take top-secret intelligence photographs.

[Spy Fact]

In 2000, the CIA built a catfish named Charlie. Charlie is a swimming robot that looks just like a real catfish. The CIA won't say why they built him. But some experts think Charlie is being used to collect water samples near suspected chemical or nuclear plants.

In this case, two military dolphins used their sonar to locate dangerous underwater mines. In the next case, dogs and gerbils use their super-sensitive noses to sniff out the bad guys.

1970-present

The Nose Knows

Can animals' superhuman sense of smell help catch drug smugglers and other bad guys?

Sniffing Out Bad Guys

A keen sense of smell makes some animals great spies and crime fighters.

People can't compare to animals when it comes to using their noses. Scientists say that a dog's sense of smell can be 44 times more sensitive than a human's.

The police, the FBI, and the military have noticed. They've enlisted animals' sensitive noses to help them solve and prevent crimes.

Dogs have been used to find hidden drugs and bombs, and even people. A dog can sniff out the trail of a child who's been missing for hours, or days.

And even a tiny gerbil can tell if you're afraid—just by sniffing the scent your body gives off. That's why gerbils have been trained to spy on suspected terrorists at the airport.

Read on to learn these animals' top-secret stories.

Max, the Wonder Dog

A very special police pooch sniffs out a hidden criminal.

In the early hours of the morning, the Alexandria, Virginia, police got a call. Someone had spotted an intruder inside a local restaurant.

The owner brought a key and let police inside the restaurant. Officer Daniel Page and his police dog, Max, started a search.

Soon, Max began scratching and growling at one corner of the room. It was a solid wall with no doors or windows nearby. Officer Page noted the area, but he saw nothing so he continued the search.

Upstairs, Max went to the same corner of the room and started to scratch and growl again. Officer Page noticed a hole in the floor. It was an airshaft that went down to

WHY ARE DOGS SUPER SNIFFERS?

Dogs' noses are built for serious smelling.

In a human nose, there are about five million scent receptors. Scent receptors tell your brain what you smell.

But dogs have 125 to 250 million scent receptors. That's 25 to 50 times the amount a human has.

What's more, the olfactory portion of a dog's brain is four times larger than a human's. The olfactory part is what understands and identifies smells.

This makes dogs' noses so sensitive they can detect even the faintest odors. A dog can smell a single drop of blood in five quarts (4.7 l) of water!

It can also smell an object that's a half mile (0.8 km) away!

Dogs are often used by law enforcement officers at crime scenes. This is Rocky, a dog that helps sniff out drugs in New York State.

the first floor. Max growled and pawed at the shaft. Clearly, he sensed something.

Officer Page pulled Max away and looked into the airshaft. There was a man hiding inside!

Max had sniffed out the intruder and had been trying to tell Officer Page all along.

The man had shimmied down the airshaft to hide—and had gotten stuck there.

Thanks to Max, the intruder was arrested. After further investigation, police learned that he had escaped from a nearby prison earlier that night.

More Super Spy Canines

The FBI, the police, and the military train dogs for many different sniffing challenges.

Max the police dog used his sensitive sense of smell to catch a restaurant intruder. Canines can also be trained to help with other undercover activities. Here are a few of them.

Tracking Dogs

Tracking dogs are used to find missing or hiding people. How do they do it?

CANINE TRAINING

Military dogs are trained deep in the heart of Texas.

Lackland Air Force Base in San Antonio, Texas, is the only place in the country that trains dogs used by the military. Even though Lackland is an air base, their dogs are used by the U.S. Army, Navy, Marine Corps, and Air Force.

Most of the dogs trained at Lackland are German shepherds and Belgian malinois. These two breeds are used because they are intelligent and hardworking. They can be trained to find explosives or drugs—or even missing people.

Each dog can cost more than $3,000 when purchased. They are usually bought from breeders in Europe. After the dogs "graduate" from Lackland, they are worth more than $11,000.

Humans shed about 40,000 dead skin cells per minute. These dead skin cells are called rafts. The rafts contain bacteria and fumes. Every person's rafts are different—just like their fingerprints are different. The wind spreads rafts into the air. That's where the tracking dog first sniffs them.

The dog follows the trail of rafts until it leads to the person with the right scent. Once the dog finds the person, it signals its handler by circling and barking, or by biting the person with the scent and holding on.

Bloodhounds have the best sense of smell of any canine. They can track a scent trail that's several days old.

Drug-Detection Dogs

Drug-detection dogs are trained to sniff out illegal substances. They work in airports, bus stations, border crossings, and seaports. They sniff people, packages, cars—anywhere drugs may be hidden. When the dog smells drugs, it alerts its handler by scratching near the source of the smell or by sitting down next to it. This signal gives the authorities the legal right to search the suspicious person, object, or area.

Explosives Detection Dogs

Instead of sniffing out drugs, these dogs are trained to find bombs. They work in airports—and are called when there's a bomb scare at a school or office building. These dogs can save lives. Once they find a bomb, humans on the bomb squad take over and **defuse** the explosive so it won't blow up.

Arson Dogs

Arson dogs are used by fire investigators. These dogs sniff for traces of gasoline or other flammable liquids used to start a fire. They make great spies because they can locate the smell of fire-starting chemicals better than the most expensive electronic device.

Judge, a bomb-sniffing dog from New York City, has been trained to detect explosives and alert the humans around him.

POINT-AND-SHOOT SPY DOGS

Canines with cameras are the latest thing in animal espionage.

At one police department in Great Britain, dogs are making videos. That's right, at the Northumbria Police Department, officers are outfitting police dogs with tiny video cameras. The project is called Firearms Intervention and Dangerous Operations—or FIDO, for short.

Canine Cameras

When a FIDO dog goes into a building, video pictures are beamed out to a handheld monitor. That lets police see if anyone dangerous is inside. The high-tech cameras are so powerful they can even see in the dark.

In the past, police tried to put cameras on dogs. But those cameras had a heavy battery pack. This meant the dogs got tired quickly. The new cameras are 75 percent lighter than the old ones. "The dogs can operate absolutely as normal and just seem to forget the camera is there," says a policeman in Northumbria.

Spy Gerbils Hunt for Terrorists!

Can the tiny super sniffers really catch bad guys at the airport?

Like dogs, gerbils have an amazing sense of smell. That's why in the 1970s, some scientists had the idea of training gerbils to catch terrorists at the airport.

The plan started when Canadian scientists learned gerbils could smell adrenaline in humans. Adrenaline is the hormone released in sweat when people are nervous. The scientists knew that terrorists would be nervous about getting caught, so their bodies would release adrenaline.

The Canadians trained the gerbils to press a lever if they detected a rise in adrenaline. Every time the gerbils correctly identified a rise in adrenaline, they were given a treat to nibble on.

An Israeli intelligence agency called the Shin Bet was the first to test the theory in a real airport. They kept some gerbils in cages next to security check points in the Tel Aviv airport. Fans blew the scent of passengers toward the gerbil cages. Whenever they smelled adrenaline, the gerbils pressed their lever.

Sounds like a good plan, right? But there was one big problem. People who are afraid of flying also get nervous and release adrenaline. The gerbils couldn't tell the difference between terrorists and passengers who were sweating simply because they were scared of flying! **24/7**

Gerbils were enlisted to sniff out nervous passengers at the Ben-Gurion Airport in Tel Aviv, Israel.

BEN-GURION AIRPORT

ANIMAL SPY

DOWNLOAD

Here's even more amazing stuff about secret agents for you to decode.

IN THIS SECTION:

▶ which military mutt shook the president's hand?

▶ how animal agents have been in the news;

▶ the tools that are used to train animals;

▶ and whether animal training might be in your future!

1

1206 Mongolian Spy Pigeons

Genghis Khan (*left*) was one of the greatest warriors who ever lived. He founded the gigantic Mongol Empire in the 1200s. Khan and his generals were among the first military men to use messenger pigeons. The birds delivered battle plans and other information to Mongol leaders fighting battles in distant areas.

Key Dates in Animal Espionage

Animals have been sticking their noses in people's business for a long time.

2

1870 Homing in on Paris

During the Franco-Prussian War, French generals trapped in the city of Paris used homing pigeons to communicate with their troops in the countryside. The pigeons were flown out of Paris in hot-air balloons (*right*). Once they reached their destinations, the pigeons were released. Secret messages were attached to their legs.

See Case #1:
Pigeons Go to War

1918 Sergeant Stubby Saves the Day!

Stubby (*below right*) was a dog that served with the U.S. 102nd Infantry in France during World War I. He could hear the whine of incoming artillery shells before humans could. So Stubby learned to bark and warn his unit of incoming poison gas attacks. After the war, President Woodrow Wilson shook Stubby's paw at the White House.

1947 Pigeon Bombers!

After World War II, British intelligence came up with a plan to train a fleet of pigeon bombers. They would attach tiny explosives to pigeons and have them fly into enemy targets.

1966 Tape Recorder Kitty

Ever hear of a spy house cat? In 1966, the CIA put a recording device inside a live feline. They called it Acoustic Kitty. The plan was that Acoustic Kitty would spy on the Russians by recording their conversations. But it never happened. Acoustic Kitty was run over by a taxi.

2003 Dolphins Are Iraq War Heroes

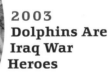

During the Iraq War, civilians didn't have enough food or medical supplies. Supply ships couldn't sail into the port because deadly mines were hidden in the water. A team of specially trained dolphins (*above*) was brought in to locate the mines.

[Spy Fact]
A "mole" is a spy working under deep cover. The name comes from the burrowing animal.

← See Case #2: Underwater Agents

In the News

Turtles Become Video Spies!

ROSTOV-ON-DON, RUSSIA—November 11, 2005

A Russian scientist has invented a device that can turn ordinary turtles into remote-controlled super spies.

Aleksey Burikovc equips a turtle's shell with a small camera. He also installs a motion sensor so that he can control the animal's movements.

This means a handler can direct the turtle in any direction he wants. The camera allows the handler to study everything that crosses the turtle's path.

Because land turtles can live without food for about a month, they can go on extended stakeouts.

They can even carry explosives, if the need ever arises.

One minor problem: They move really, really slowly!

Could this turtle become a spy? It could if scientist Aleksey Burikovc put one of his turtle cams on it.

These bomb-sniffing honeybees are resting in a custom-designed harness at the Los Alamos National Laboratory. When they're on duty, they can detect explosives that are difficult—or dangerous—for dogs to investigate.

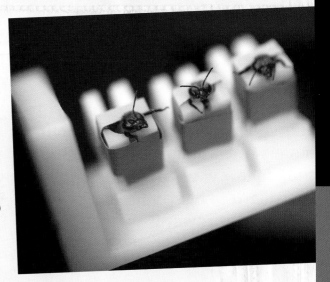

Bees Can Sniff Out Bombs!

LOS ALAMOS, NEW MEXICO—November 28, 2005

Military scientists have found a way to train bees to sniff out explosives used in bombs. This program was developed to help protect American troops in Iraq, say scientists from the Los Alamos National Laboratory in New Mexico. Roadside bombs in Iraq have killed many soldiers and innocent civilians.

"Scientists have long marveled at the honeybee's phenomenal sense of smell, which rivals that of dogs," said Tim Haarmann, principal investigator of the project. Bees could sniff out bomb locations that are too difficult or dangerous for dogs to get to.

Animal Boot Camp

The trick to training animals is to give them positive reinforcement. This means rewarding them with food when they follow your commands. Over time, they learn to obey you—so they'll keep getting that reward!

TRAINING A HOMING PIGEON

Your pigeon will need to live in a loft like this one.

Step 1: Leaving the Loft

When the pigeon is between six and eight weeks old, let it out of its loft for the first time. But only let it out when it's hungry.

Step 2: Training the Pigeon to Return

When you want the pigeon to return, blow a whistle.

Your whistle will give off a single shrill note that your pigeon will learn to recognize.

Step 3: Give the Pigeon Positive Reinforcement

As soon as the pigeon returns, feed it. That's **positive reinforcement**—a reward. The pigeon will learn to return to the loft whenever it hears the whistle. It wants its reward.

Pigeon food is usually made up of field peas, popcorn, milo, heard wheat, red millet, white millet, canary grass seeds, rice, and hemp seed.

Step 4: Increase the Distance

Next, train the pigeon to return home from greater distances. Start by taking it two to three miles (3.2 to 4.8 km) from the loft and releasing it. Next time, take the pigeon five miles (8 km), then ten miles (16 km), then 15 miles (24 km).

Step 5: Develop Its Sense of Direction

Finally, release the pigeon from a different direction each time—north, south, east, and west. This teaches it to find its way home no matter where it is.

Not sure which way's up? A compass can help you determine direction. Inside is a rotating magnetic needle that always points north.

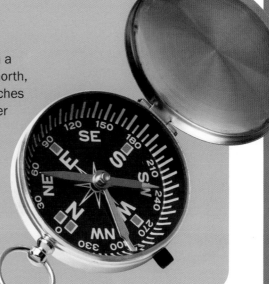

TRAINING A DOLPHIN

If you want to train a marine mammal, you've got to get in the water. A wet suit can keep you warm while you're training.

Step 1: Give the Dolphin a Command

Say or signal a command for the dolphin to do something, like swim toward you.

Trainers may use scuba gear if they're going to be underwater for a long time. This equipment can include a snorkel, diving mask, air tank, and rebreather.

Step 2: Build a Bridge

If the dolphin performs the command correctly, give it a signal. Blow a whistle, or say a word like "Good!" This signal is called a **bridge**. Make sure you communicate the bridge at the exact moment the dolphin follows the command. That way the dolphin learns to link the bridge with the command.

Step 3: Give the Dolphin Positive Reinforcement

When the dolphin completes the command, give it some positive reinforcement—like a treat.

Dolphins should get a reward every time they follow the command correctly. And for dolphins, that treat should be fish.

TRAINING A DRUG DOG

Drug dogs start by finding towels. Towels hold scents well, and they're easy to hide.

Step 1: **Scent a Towel**

Scent a towel with the odor of a drug. Trainers often use a chemical called "pseudo drugs." *Pseudo* means fake or pretend. Hide the scented towel from the dog.

Step 2: **Give the Dog a Command**

Command the dog to find the scented towel.

One or two of these will keep the dog interested in the task.

Step 3: **Give the Dog Positive Reinforcement**

When the dog finds the scented towel, give it some positive reinforcement.

Step 4: **Make it Tough**

Make it harder for the dog to sniff out the drugs by placing the towel in a sealed container. Continue to give the dog harder challenges each time. Of course, reward the dog with a treat each time it succeeds!

Sometimes both the trainer and the drug dog wear vests to identify themselves as a working team.

51

HELP WANTED:
Animal Trainer

Interested in the world of animal training? Here's more information about the field.

Q&A: SHANNON DAISEY

Shannon Daisey is a marine mammal trainer at the National Aquarium in Baltimore.

24/7: What's a typical day at work like for you?

SHANNON DAISEY: There are generally two shifts here: "food prep" and "late shift." When on the food preparation shift, we arrive at 6:30 A.M. and begin thawing and bucketing out about 200 pounds (90 kg) of frozen fish into each of the eight dolphins' buckets. Each dolphin gets ten buckets of fish daily!

At around 8 A.M., we begin training sessions every hour or so. During training sessions, we play, swim, practice behaviors, train new behaviors, and build relationships with the dolphins.

We train and practice many behaviors so that the dolphins can voluntarily participate in their medical care. Our dolphins are trained to give voluntary blood, gastric, fecal, urine, milk, and blowhole samples.

The late shift leaves between 6 and 9 P.M. each night. We perform three or four 25-minute educational shows each day and several poolside programs with guests each week.

24/7: What is your favorite thing about being a dolphin trainer?

DAISEY: Observing how the dolphins learn new behaviors. It's exhilarating to see the moment when "the lightbulb goes off" and they get it.

It's also very rewarding to teach children about efforts to protect wild animals. It's great to be there when a child is first inspired by these amazing creatures. I wake up every day and am excited to go to work.

24/7: Do you have any advice for young adults who would like to become marine mammal trainers?

DAISEY: Get a bachelor's degree in biology, psychology, or any science-related field. Be able to swim pretty well. Obtain your scuba certification. Have good interpersonal teamwork skills and be able to take and give constructive criticism very graciously. We are all always learning, no matter how long we have worked in the field.

Most important, volunteer and/or intern at any animal care facility. Work really hard and don't be afraid to show you can get dirty and scrub and clean a lot! It is also the best way to find out if this really is the job for you.

THE STATS:

DAY JOB: Animal trainers can work in zoos, circuses, horse stables, dog obedience schools, or law enforcement agencies. Many animal trainers also hold other animal-related jobs. Some are breeders, veterinary technicians, or zookeepers.

EDUCATION:
▶ Dog handlers must to go through a special program and become certified.
▶ Marine mammal trainers usually earn a four-year bachelor's degree.
▶ Veterinarians need a bachelor's degree plus four years of veterinary school.

SKILLS: Dog handlers must feed, walk, and clean up after their dogs. The handler must also make sure their dogs are healthy—and call a veterinarian if one is not.

Marine mammal trainers need excellent swimming skills and physical strength. They are usually outdoors in all kinds of weather.

DO YOU HAVE WHAT IT TAKES?

Take this totally unscientific quiz to see if animal training might be a good career for you.

1 Do you like to be outside?
a) Yes, I play outdoors in the summer or winter.
b) I like it, but I like being inside, too.
c) Nah, I'd much rather watch TV.

2 Do you love zoos and aquariums?
a) I try to spend all my free time there.
b) I like the zoo—when I'm not at the movies.
c) There are too many animals. And the smell bugs me!

3 Do you have any pets?
a) Just my dogs, cats, fish, mice, and chickens!
b) I feed my brother's puppy sometimes.
c) I had a goldfish—but it died!

4 Are you patient when you explain things?
a) Yes, I like to get things right.
b) Sometimes yes, sometimes no.
c) URGGGH. I'm annoyed already!

5 Are animal shows your favorite thing on TV?
a) Yes, I record every program on Animal Planet.
b) I'll watch them if they're on.
c) There are animal shows on TV?

YOUR SCORE
Give yourself 3 points for every "a" you chose. Give yourself 2 points for every "b" you chose. Give yourself 1 point for every "c" you chose.

If you got **13–15 points**, you're a born animal trainer.
If you got **10–12 points**, working with animals is a career option.
If you got **5–9 points**, you might want to look at another career.

HOW TO GET STARTED...NOW!

It's never too early to start working toward your goals.

GET AN EDUCATION
- Focus on your science classes, especially biology.
- Start thinking about college. Look for ones with good animal biology or veterinary programs.
- Read the newspaper. Keep up with what's going on in your community.
- Read anything you can find about animal programs and training.
- Graduate from high school!

NETWORK!
Find out about animal groups in your area. See if you can find a local Society for the Prevention of Cruelty to Animals (SPCA) worker, veterinarian, or zookeeper who might be willing to give you advice.

GET AN INTERNSHIP
Look for an internship with a veterinarian or at a local zoo or aquarium. Or volunteer with the SPCA in your town.

LEARN ABOUT OTHER JOBS WORKING WITH ANIMALS
Animal trainers can work in zoos, aquariums, aviaries, amusement and theme parks, circuses, horse stables, dog obedience schools, and law enforcement agencies. Some train animals for competition, the film industry, and services for the disabled. Many work other jobs, too. They can be veterinarians or breeders, for example.

Resources

Looking for more information about animal training? Here are some resources you don't want to miss!

PROFESSIONAL ORGANIZATIONS

American Zoo and Aquarium Association (AZA)
www.aza.org
8403 Colesville Road, Suite 710
Silver Spring, MD 20910
PHONE: 301-562-0777
FAX: 301-562-0888

The AZA promotes animal care, wildlife conservation, education, and science. It accredits zoos and aquariums throughout the United States.

International Association of Avian Trainers and Educators (IAATE)
www.iaate.org
350 St. Andrews Fairway
Memphis, TN 38111
PHONE: 901-685-9122
FAX: 901-685-7233

The IAATE works to promote education for and communication among avian trainers and other professionals.

International Marine Animal Trainers Association
www.imata.org
1200 South Lake Shore Drive
Chicago, IL 60605

This organization helps instruct professionals who train marine animals and is dedicated to the humane care and handling of those animals.

North American Police Work Dog Association
www.napwda.com
4222 Manchester Avenue
Perry, OH 44081
PHONE: 888-4CANINE

This group provides training and workshops for police dogs throughout North America.

U.S. Customs Service's Canine Enforcement Training Center
www.customs.ustreas.gov/xp/cgov
/enforcement/canines/
1300 Pennsylvania Avenue NW
Washington, DC 20229
PHONE: 888-USA-DOG1
E-MAIL: canine@dhs.gov

This organization trains dogs who work at airports and along U.S. borders.

U.S. Navy Marine Mammal Program (NMMP)
www.spawar.navy.mil/sandiego/tec
hnology/mammals/index.html
San Diego, CA
PHONE: 619-553-2717

This division of the U.S. Navy trains dolphins and other marine animals for detecting mines, object recovery, and other projects.

U.S. Police Canine Association (USPCA)
www.uspcak9.com
P.O. Box 80
Springboro, OH 45066
PHONE: 800-531-1614

This organization was formed when the Police K-9 Association and the United States K-9 Association merged. It works to standardize dog training and promote the use of canines in law enforcement.

Work Dogs International
www.policedogtrainers.com/
43455 Hilltop Drive
Banning, CA 92220
PHONE: 951-922-3700

Work Dogs International is a worldwide organization that trains dogs for police work and bomb detection.

WEB SITES

FBI: Working Dogs
www.fbi.gov/kids/dogs/know.htm

For an explanation of how dogs work for the FBI.

Global Intelligence News Portal
mprofaca.cro.net/spycats.html

Provides information on Acoustic Kitty's mission.

International Herald Tribune: The Hallowed History of the Carrier Pigeon
www.iht.com/articles/2004/
01/30/blume_ed3__1.php

To learn more about pigeons during wartime.

International Spy Museum
www.spymuseum.org/index.asp

To learn about both human and animals spies throughout history.

National Geographic News: Dogs at War
news.nationalgeographic.com/new
s/2003/04/0409_030409_mili-
tarydogs.html

For information about how canines are used by the military.

57

National Geographic News: Dolphins Deployed as Undersea Agents in Iraq
news.nationalgeographic.com/ news/2003/03/0328_030328_ wardolphins_2.html

To learn more about the work dolphins are doing in the Iraq War.

Overview of Careers in Animal Training
http://www3.ccps.virginia.edu/ career_prospects/briefs/P-S/SummaryAnimalTrain.shtml

To learn more about a career in animal training.

Scholastic News: Rebuilding Iraq
teacher.scholastic.com/ scholasticnews/indepth/war-iraq/ during_war/index.asp?article= dolphins

To read an article about the dolphins who cleared the way for ships to enter the port of Umm Qasr.

U.S. Department of Labor: Animal Care and Service Workers
www.bls.gov/oco/ocos168.htm

For information about what animal trainers do.

BOOKS

Cerullo, Mary. Dolphins: *What They Can Teach Us*. New York: Dutton Juvenile, 1997.

Felber, Bill. *The Horse in War* (The Horse Library). Broomall, Pa.: Chelsea House, 2001.

George, Isabel, and Rob Lloyd Jones. *Animals at War*. London: Usborne Books, 2007.

Miller, Marie-Therese. *Helping Dogs* (Dog Tales: True Stories About Amazing Dogs). New York: Chelsea House, 2007.

Patent, Dorothy Hinshaw. *Pigeons*. New York: Clarion Books, 1997.

Presnall, Judith Janda. *Canine Companions* (Animals with Jobs). San Diego: KidHaven Press, 2003.

Presnall, Judith Janda. *Navy Dolphins* (Animals with Jobs). San Diego: KidHaven Press, 2001.

Ruffin, Frances E. *Military Dogs* (Dog Heroes). New York: Bearport Publishing, 2006.

Sandler, Michael. *Military Horses* (Horse Power). New York: Bearport Publishing, 2007.

A

adrenaline (uh-DREN-uh-lun) *noun* a hormone that kicks in when someone is excited or nervous; it makes a person's energy level and blood pressure rise and can make a person sweat

agent (AY-juhnt) *noun* a person or animal who collects information and performs other secret tasks on behalf of an intelligence service like the CIA

allies (AL-eyes) *noun* the "good guys"; the people or groups on your side

artillery (ar-TIH-lur-ee) *noun* weapons, usually mounted guns and rockets, or those used to launch missiles

B

barrage (buh-RAHZ) *noun* artillery fire shot close to friendly troops to screen and protect them

bridge (bridj) *noun* a signal that indicates a command has been correctly followed

C

CIA (see-eye-AY) *noun* an agency of the U.S. government that deals with foreign intelligence (the secrets and knowledge of other countries) and counterintelligence (misleading spies from other countries). It stands for *Central Intelligence Agency*.

clicks (kliks) *noun* pulses of sound sent out by dolphins

Cold War (kold war) *noun* the period after World War II when communist countries, such as the Soviet Union, and noncommunist countries, such as the United States, were competing against one another

counterintelligence (kown-tur-in-TEL-uh-juhnss) *noun* organized activity that catches spies or blocks the transfer of information between spies and intelligence agencies

D

defuse (dee-FYOOZ) *verb* to remove the fuse from a bomb or mine

detect (deh-TEKT) *verb* to discover that something exists or is present

DHS (DEE-aych-ess) *noun* a U.S. government agency that is responsible for protecting the country. It stands for *Department of Homeland Security*.

Dictionary

DIA (DEE-eye-ay) *noun* a branch of the U.S. Department of Defense that provides support for the U.S. military. It stands for *Defense Intelligence Agency*.

E

echoes (EH-koze) *noun* repetitions of sound

echolocation (eh-koh-loh-KAY-shun) *noun* a system of detecting objects by using a pattern of sound waves

enemy (EN-uh-mee) *noun* the "bad guys"; the side you're fighting against

espionage (ESS-pee-uh-nahzh) *noun* the act of spying or the work of a spy

evacuate (ih-VA-kyoo-ate) *verb* to leave or withdraw, usually for protection

F

FBI (eff-bee-EYE) *noun* a U.S. government agency that fights terrorism and organized crime. It stands for the *Federal Bureau of Investigation*.

H

handler (HAN-dler) *noun* a person responsible for training and caring for animals

homing pigeon (HOH-ming PIH-juhn) *noun* a breed of pigeon that naturally returns to its nest no matter where it is taken

I

intelligence (in-TEL-uh-juhnss) *noun* information gained by spying

intercept (in-tur-SEPT) *verb* to stop or seize something before it can reach its intended destination

invade (in-VAYD) *verb* to enter, with hopes of controlling a certain area or place

M

magnetic pull (mag-NEH-tik pul) *noun* a force that attracts magnetic objects to one another

marine mammals (muh-REEN MA-muls) *noun* mammals that live in the water

melons (MEH-luns) *noun* structures inside a dolphin's brain that send out pulses of sound

mines (mines) *noun* explosive devices that can be hidden in the ground or underwater

mission (MIH-shun) *noun* a special job or task

N

NSA (en-ess-AY) *noun* a branch of the U.S. Department of Defense that is responsible for the security of U.S. government communications. It stands for *National Security Agency*.

nuclear weapons (NOO-klee-ur WEH-punz) *noun* missiles and other weapons that are made from nuclear reactions and can cause incredible damage

P

positive reinforcement (POZ-uh-tiv ree-in-FORS-muhnt) *noun* a system of encouraging good behavior through rewards and praise

R

rafts (rafts) *noun* large groups of dead skin cells that fall off a person's body

recruited (reh-KROOT-ed) *verb* hired, secured, or convinced members to join a group

S

scent receptors (sent rih-SEP-turz) *noun* the sensitive places inside the nose that tell your brain what you smell

sensors (SEN-surz) *noun* devices that detect physical qualities such as heat, smell, light, sound, or motion

siege (seezh) *noun* a military blockade of a city or other area, in hopes of making it surrender

sonar (SO-nahr) *noun* a way of locating objects underwater by using sound waves

spy (spye) *noun* a person or animal who tries to secretly get or send information

T

terrorists (TAIR-ur-ists) *noun* people who try to control others through violence, usually for political reasons

Index

always knew that dogs were used by police. And I knew that the military used dolphins in the Persian Gulf. But it wasn't until I began researching this book that I realized just how many other animals have served as spies!

If you search Google for the term "spy animal" you won't find much information. Most of the animals discussed in this book were never really referred to as "spies." They were called military animals or service animals. The phrase "animals in war" turns up quite a lot of links, because it is in times of war that animals are often called to duty.

In the process of writing this book, I also learned that many animals have died in war. So many animals, in fact, that there are memorials for them. Sad, but true. Just like the soldiers who sacrifice for us, many animals have been battlefield heroes.

ACKNOWLEDGMENTS

would like to thank the experts who contributed to this book. Their time, effort, and expertise were invaluable to its creation. I would also like to thank Kate Waters, Suzanne Harper, Jennifer Wilson, Elizabeth Ward, and Katie Marsico for their support.

CREDITS: Daniel Page, Retired Canine Officer, Alexandria, Virginia, Police Department

CONTENT ADVISER: Steven Aftergood, Director of the Project on Government Secrecy, Federation of American Scientists

Photo Credits: Photographs © 2008: age fotostock: 49 top (Brand X Pictures), 11 bottom (Pablo Galán Cela), 4 bottom, 8 (Comstock Images), 50 top (Rubberball Production); AP Images: 28 (Wilfredo Lee), 48 top (Charlie Neibergall), 55 (Amy Sancetta), 42 (Ariel Schalit), 3 (Bob Zellar/Billings Gazette); Boston University, Photo Services: 34; Bruce Coleman Inc./David Falconer: 22; Corbis Images: 6 top, 14 top, 18, 44 top, 45 top (Bettmann), 5 bottom, 39 (DLILLC), 5 top, 16, 19 top (Hulton-Deutsch Collection), 40 (Peter Morgan/Reuters), 15; DK Images: 1, 2 (Jane Burton), 48 bottom; Getty Images: 14 bottom center (Terry Ashe), 51 bottom (Jay Directo), 10 top (John Edwards), 4 top, 11 top (Mark Harwood), 24 (Spencer Platt), 14 center, 20 bottom (Paul J. Richards), 35 (Andersen Ross), 47 (Rick Scibelli), 51 top (Stockbyte), 14 top center (Mark Wilson), 14 bottom (Alex Wong); Index Stock Imagery: 6 bottom, 51 center (Dan Gair Photographic), 46 (Jeff Greenberg); International Spy Museum: cover; IStockphoto/Eric Isselee: back cover; JupiterImages/Ross Pictures: 50 bottom; National Aquarium, Baltimore/George Grall: 52; NEWSCOM/Cara Owsley/Biloxi Sun Herald: 5 center, 25; Peter Arnold Inc./BIOS Klein & Hubert: 11 center; Photodisc, Inc./via SODA: 49 bottom; Reuters/Sin Walker/POOL: 45 bottom; Smithsonian Institution, Washington, DC/Jeff Tinsley: 20 top; Superstock, Inc./Stuart Westmorland/age fotostock: 10 bottom; The Image Works: 44 bottom (ARPL/HIP), 38 (David Lassman/Syracuse Newspapers), 44 bottom; U.S. Navy Photo: 31, 33 (Brien Aho), 27, 29 (Bob Houlihan). Maps by David Lindroth, Inc.